Historical Album

— of —

East Tennessee

1898

Charles A. Reeves, Jr.

A reproduction of a booklet originally published by W. A. J. Moore

FIRST CAPITOL OF THE STATE.
Cumberland and State Streets. Knoxville.

Charles A. Reeves, Jr.
Technical Illustration & Publishing
Specializing in Cartography and Genealogy

10812 Dineen Drive   (865) 966-5768
Knoxville, Tennessee 37934-1809
e-mail: reevesca@tds.net
Home Page: http://ReevesMaps.com

ISBN 978-0-9800984-5-7

How this booklet was produced: Charles' original copy was scanned at 300 dpi and the images edited in Adobe Photoshop to remove artifacts. The pages were scanned in color, although the original photographs were black-and-white. They were then converted to greyscale for this printing.

Note: The original format of this booklet was horizontal. Because of printing limiations, the format for this version has been revised to vertical, requiring some editorial changes from the original.

Historical Album

......OF......

EAST TENNESSEE

~1898~

Price 25 Cents.

Copyright 1898
By W. A. J. MOORE,
Knoxville, Tenn.

KNOXVILLE WHEN A VILLAGE.

Knoxville Furniture Co.

Knoxville, = = Tennessee.

Manufacturers of

Artistic Wood Mantels and Bed=Room Suites.

The trade of Mantel and Furniture Dealers solicited.

Illustrated Catalogues sent to dealers only, upon application.

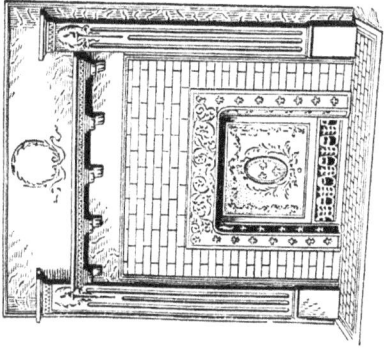

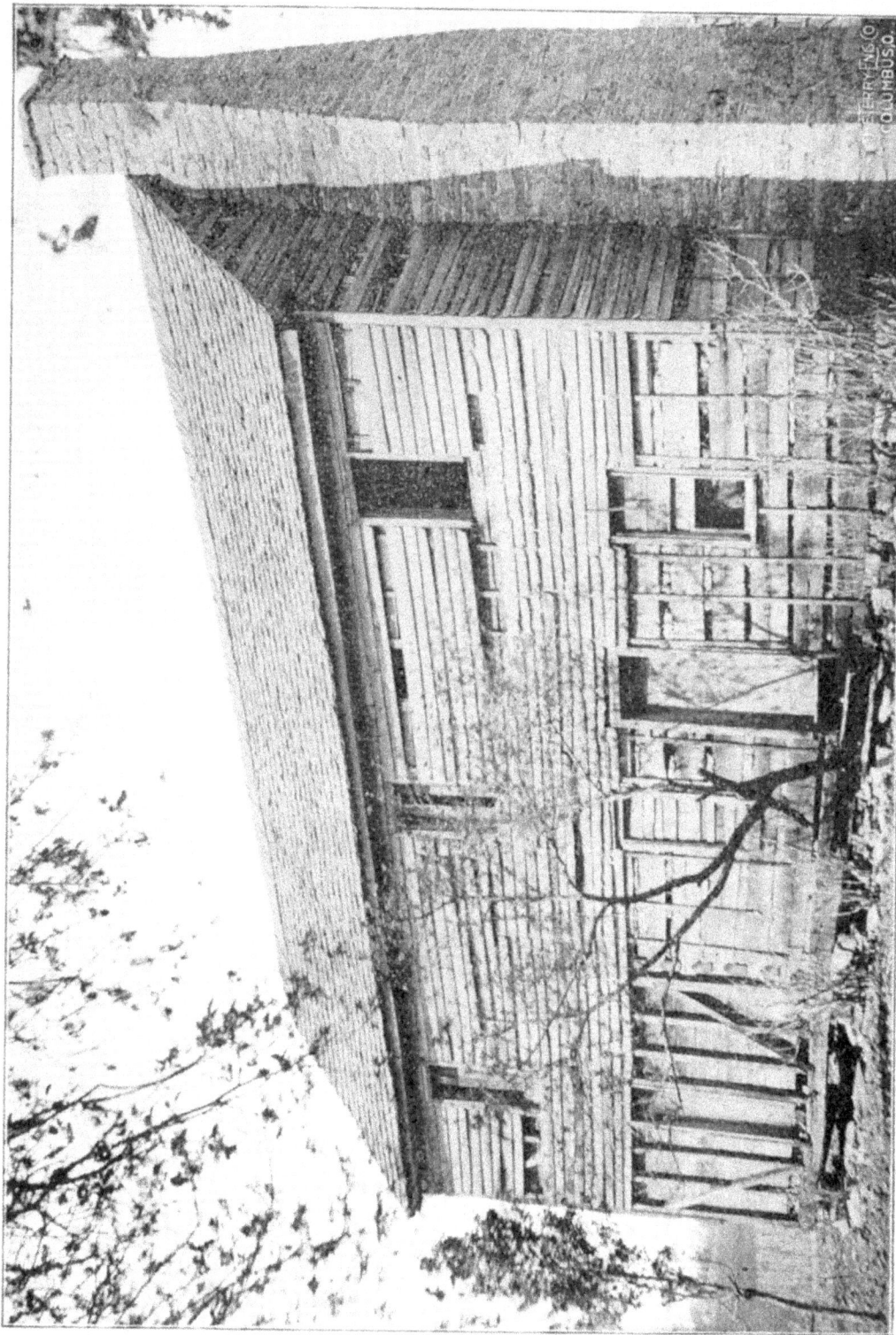

GOV. SEVIER'S RESIDENCE

Now standing on Nola Chucky River, 10 miles south of Jonesboro, Washington County, Tenn.

BUILDING IN WHICH GOV. SEVIER WAS CAPTURED BY CAPT. TIPTON in 1788, when accused of treason and trying to escape into North Carolina. The building stands in Washington County, 7 miles from Jonesboro.

GOV. SEVIER'S OLD HOME PLACE.
Near Neubert's Springs.

GOV. SEVIER'S OLD SMOKE HOUSE,
Near Neubert's Springs, Knox County.

OLD DWELLING NEAR BELL'S BRIDGE, KNOX COUNTY,
was attacked by Indians when occupied by the great uncle of the present owner.
Erected about 1795.

TOMBSTONE OF JACOB BROWN.
First white man buried in Tennessee. 9 miles from Jonesboro, Washington County,
Accidentally killed while bear hunting.

OLD TIME EAST TENNESSEE CORN CRACKER.

OLD TIME SCHOOL HOUSE—STILL IN USE.

MRS. NANCY JONES,

One of the Five Revolutionary Pensioners now living, about 88 years of age.   Resides near Jonesboro.

FIRST CAPITOL OF THE STATE.
Cumberland and State Streets, Knoxville.

PRESENT STATE CAPITOL, NASHVILLE.

CHANDLER BROS.

—SUCCESSORS TO—

THE KNOXVILLE SUPPLY CO.

—DEALERS IN—

Black Diamond and Portland Cement, Sewer Pipe, Drain Tile, Fire Brick, Fire Clay, Flue Pipe, Lath, Hair, Plaster Paris, Ready Roofing and Building Papers.

✿ ✿ ✿ ✿ ✿

—CONTRACTORS FOR—

Portland Cement Walks, Floors, and Gravel Roofs.

✿ ✿ ✿ ✿ ✿

421 W. Depot St.   Telephones 385.

KNOXVILLE, TENN.

ENTERPRISE MACHINE WORKS.

D. C. RICHARDS & SONS,

Founders and Machinists.

Heavy Gearing and Hoisting Machinery for Mines and Quarries.

LOCOMOTIVE WORK A SPECIALTY.

NEW COUNTY BRIDGE ACROSS TENNESSEE RIVER AT KNOXVILLE.

Completed July 1st, 1898. 1690 feet in length, 42 feet in width, 165 feet above low water mark, cost, all complete, $27,500.

UNIVERSITY OF TENNESSEE DURING THE CIVIL WAR.
Barracks in the Background.

BIRTHPLACE OF ADMIRAL FARRAGUT, LOWE'S FERRY, KNOX COUNTY.
He was born 1801, in a house which stood a few feet from this building.

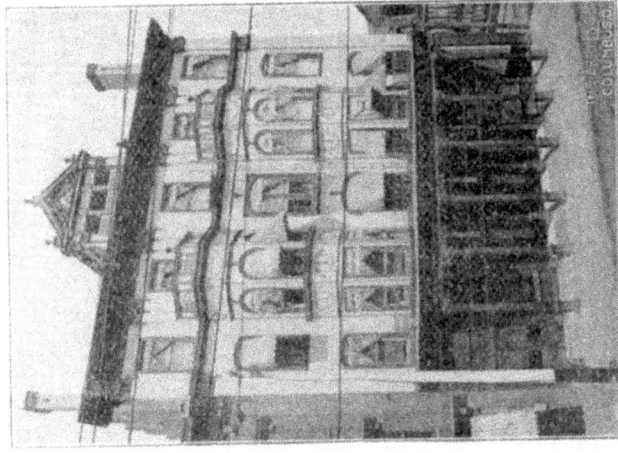

STONE BUILDING SIX MILES EAST OF KNOXVILLE.

Erected in North Carolina and has stood during the history of the States of Franklin and Tennessee.

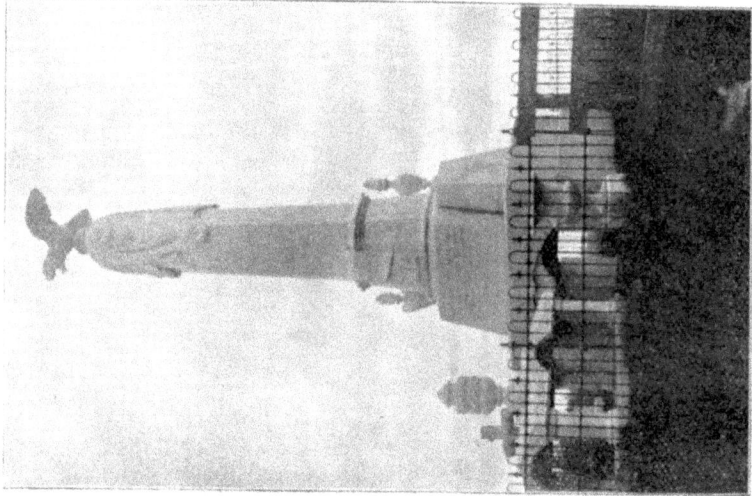

PRESIDENT JOHNSON'S RESIDENCE, GREENEVILLE, TENN.

PARSON BROWNLOW'S PRINTING OFFICE AND RESIDENCE,
Jonesboro, Tenn., in which he conducted Henry Clay's Presidential campaign, 1844.

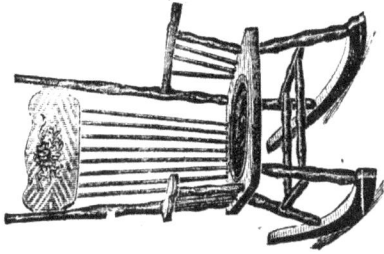

PARSON BROWNLOW'S RESIDENCE.

Cumberland Street, Knoxville, where his Widow now Lives.